To Vanessa,
I hope you enjoy
reading.

[signature]

The Light
from Within

WRITTEN AND ILLUSTRATED BY

NANCY W. KELLEY

ISBN 978-1-64079-323-1 (paperback)
ISBN 978-1-64114-968-6 (hardcover)
ISBN 978-1-64079-324-8 (digital)

Christian Faith Publishing, Inc.
832 Park Avenue
Meadville, PA 16335
www.christianfaithpublishing.com

Printed in the United States of America

This book is dedicated to the Center for Loss and Bereavement, specifically Steve Keller for setting me north, Emily Vincent for her insight through the hard times, and Clair Drexler for offering me a new perspective. To my family and friends who have listened, understood, been a part of this journey, shared their own wisdom, and have each in their own way, contributed to the fulfillment of my life more than I can express.

A gifted hand

God has given me
To bring forth
That which forsakes thee
For each experience
At its core
Is a God-given difficult chore

God,
My dear, you sure do test

Do I dare ask God
To provide for me
As if, dear God, can it really be
A worthy me to share your word

I now have this gift of pen
Problem is
I want revenge

In His Shadow

Put one foot in front of the other
Every day
And pray to God while on your way
For in his shadow you do walk
And all the while
You still balk
To ask of God
To take away
Any pain of a given day
It's up to you and God alone
To say a prayer and then atone
Answer prayers he does do
Believing in the outcome
Is up to you

When the rug comes
out from under
It's easy to question
Was this my blunder
I wonder, I wonder
So hard it is to recover
When the rug comes
out from under
They take your job
And paycheck too
I wonder now
What am I gonna do

Worry, Worry All Day Long

Every morning I feel like crying
It gets so hard to keep on trying
How do I try, who really knows
I just get up and thumb my nose
Another day, the Lord has provided
It seems I'm just divided
Never really give him my hand
To lead me on his wondrous plan

Survival is a word
Which rhymes with *rival*
The intertwined words are like any great battle
Hold on to the reins
Go through the pain
Perhaps you will see yourself again
Survival
is the test of time
Of strength and endurance
Which strengthens the mind

The Love in Our Hearts

The pebble goes in, the ripples go out
Why do I see this in my mind's eye
So sick you were, I wanted to cry
With love and compassion I wanted to be
Instead anxiety made it all about me
The love in our hearts, it is for certain
Even as God closes the curtain
The pebble goes in, the ripples go out
This is what love is all about

The Wicked One

Hats and scarfs we did buy
To cover your heads
So you won't cry
Feeling beautiful in the midst of
Disease
It's so important for you to believe
A beautiful person you still are
Don't worry, my love, it's just a scar
A touch of cancer, they do say
Who would believe it's here to stay
Drugs they give you
Which make you sick
Here, my dear, just one more prick
The drugs they save you
And make it so
To save your life from a wicked foe

Two Chairs

You got hurt just like him
Oh my Lord, it feels like a sin
Off to the hospital we do rush,
Tomorrow morning,
My tears just gush
To see for ourselves, can this be true
My dear God, what are we to do?
Two of my brothers now in a chair
Lord, have mercy, this isn't fair

Dear Fear,

You are no friend
Listen, listen, you have no end

Over and over in my head
Same old thing day after day
Over and over in my head
Same old, same old
Dread, dread, dread

Fear of what
My daily chore?
Seems the truth
I just want more
It's the same old fear
As it was before

Fear of nothing
That's the truth

Every day is the Lord's proof

The Resilient One

The resilient one, it makes me shiver
Of all these things, I did quiver
Resilient not because I've won
The stuff of life is never done

The stranger that I know

Is every Tom, Dick, Harry, and Joe
Don't really know them
But to say hello
Have a good day,
That's all there is for today
Make up stories to be familiar
I wonder if their life is at all similar
I'm not really interested in being a friend
With the person to whom I pretend
For every person is a Tom, Dick, Harry, and Joe
You could just be
The very stranger
that they know

Grace, you know,

Lives across the street
Such a neat lady
And a person you should meet
To know her is a mystery
She keeps to herself
But is so full of history
A God-loving woman
This is for sure
She sends me flowers
Which I adore!

Long time ago, I knew a friend

But thirty years we did spend
Out of touch and on our own
Raising children and growing older,
Rushing around as Americans do
We've lived our lives inside our homes
You've lost touch with those dear friends
But from time to time, they come to mind
I must reach out to this friend of mine
The days go by, and the years do too
By the time you look up, twenty years
You've gone through
The youngest of children have now left the nest
All of a sudden, you have a new test
Catching up is now the chore,
It seems as though you still adore
The very friend who you knew back when

Many a wonderful mother

I have had the honor to know
The gifts of our hearts
We truly do sow
A wonderful mother,
Can sit and observe
Or perhaps let this child
Get on our nerves
A mother knows the truth
If she is open to suggestion
That perhaps this latest event
Is our very own lesson

My loves as it was meant to be

From the day God gave each of you to me
Each of you in your own way
Brightens my every day
My three girlies
Are a pearly gem
A magnet for all the men
I knew you with your crooked teeth
And the nights when you couldn't sleep
Off on your bike you did go
Where you went, I'll never really know
Up in a tree, there you are
How in the world did you get so far
Sing like a bird
And so I have heard!
I know
all parents feel the same
But you haven't met them,
You don't know their names

The Master Craftsman

The youngest of seven
Where in the world
are you headin'?

So defiant all the time
Why can't you just
be to dinner on time

The most rebellious of us all
Is it because you were very small?

The master craftsman pursued his dream
Even when it didn't seem

A certain path for our kind of folk
It seemed as though you wanted to provoke

He could build a chest
Of rounded corner

One in which was inspired
Only from the spirit which lays inside

A hope chest of circular means
Was the most beautiful chest
I have ever seen

The Elusive One

I've dubbed him Mr. Big
He lives in a Ville
Only about six hours up the hill
Many a year has been spent there
But we all know
Exactly where!
So many friends and he has many
Going on years as few as twenty
They take care of him
And love him as a brother
But the truth is
I'm the daughter of his mother
Elusive he is and elusive he will be
Until the time
We see him again,
And say
Hey there,
How you be?

Senility

Remember my name, you can't recall
I remember when you were once tall
Memories which have been taken away
Senility, it's here to stay
Fishing, swimming, and cooking worms
Do you remember how they squirmed
Some days you are here, and some days not
I think of the memories you forgot
Once in awhile you present
To remind us of the life you spent
All of a sudden, you appear
Look it's him who is so dear
Back to the abyss
I must remember this
You are not the person
Whom I miss

So Strong

I have never seen a woman so strong
You took care of him for so very long
He was wonderful and so very bright
You looked upon him with such delight
Feed him, bathe him, and laugh all along
My God, woman, you are so strong
I hear the laughter from upstairs
Thirty years you did spare
Laughing, crying, having fun
Today with you, he will sit in the sun
Your faith, it kept you from despair
Your love, we knew, was always there
Loving and kind, with such compassion
I didn't realize this was your passion
To share his life for so long
My God, woman, you are so strong
I love you, Mom!

The Dishes

The cycles of life, it's hard to believe
One can stutter or roll up your sleeve
One day you're here
The next day not
One way or another
Give your best shot
The dirty dishes are in the sink
You wish them away
With a long, long blink
Here to stay the dishes are
To leave them there
Well, that's bizarre
Where have I been all these years
I've wasted so many on unhappy tears
Tears, they came and then they went
As each life's lesson did present
I did not know of what to do
But just kept trying through and through
My peace today,
It comes from within
I move along with a happy grin
The dishes are clean and put away
In hopes to use them another day

Hurry, hurry
It's the lightning bugs
Quick, run in the house and
Get us a jug
I'll stay out
And be the scout

The lightning bugs are
All about

Did you ever scare yourself
From something that just can't be
Like swimming in a pool
Oh so free

Here come the sharks
From over there

Quick, run out 'cause now
I'm scared

Swimming, swimming in the pool
Quick, jump in and get real cool
Down to the bottom and up to the top
I don't think I'm ever gonna stop
Around the pool I do go
Getting dipped from head to toe
Keep on going
You're almost there
Around the top
Now down the side
I think of the shark again
I simply can't hide

Instant Messaging

I M me all day long
Happy now to sing the song
Of a fantasy not meant to be
Boy, oh boy,
Wish I were free
Today is done,
It's time for home
Can't wait till tomorrow
When we can roam
In pretend,
It's only to be
The idea of you and me

Compassion, compassion

We ration, we ration
Far easier it is to stay inside
Than to help those
To whom we can oblige

Ration my compassion a daily event
So much time,
Easier spent
On the way from here to there
Dear God,
Can I really spare
A kind word or deed
To help a fellow in need.

The Invalid

When you see me in this bed
Why do you look at me with such dread
My muscles can't move
Now don't you see
Get up now and make me some
Tea!
Give it here, now don't you spill
Over there is my other pill
Bend the straw to give me a sip
Ooopsy, now there's a drip!
Down my face it does go
Hurry on, you are so slow
I want to sit and just be calm
Before we reach another dawn
Up I go to do some more
Here, my love, is another chore

you
are
Loved
by
many

The Deserter

I once knew a man so handsome and smart,
But he's taken off and has broken my heart.
Thirty years we did spend, raising our children through
To the end

He took off
So selfish, you know,
He left me to tender what he didn't sow
Now he holds me in contempt, you see
Because he believes it was all me

I loved him so deeply for all those
Years, but now my life is full of tears

Fear
I struggle every day to hope in a life that seems
Far away.

I face the struggles of a single mom, then life
Gives a big turn like a great big bomb
I'm forced to make decisions so hard, it's true

The kids, they are dear
and wonderful too

They must know my love is true

I move forward in a most arduous way
And hope in a Lord that is not far away.

My God, I know you love me,
For I am blessed today
I give you all my hopes and dreams
To move my life through winding streams

Insidious

Off to work I do go
Work, ya know, well, it's just so
Happy I am to be at this place
I'm even happy to see your face
A good man you seem to be
Until you turn the tables on me
For some strange reason,
You decide
This here girl could hurt your pride
So easy it is for you to chide
I tell ya now,
I won't abide
God, cover me with your loving hand
So I can learn to really stand
Against the enemy I now do face
This is now a long, long race
Up against him I do go
To the tell the boss of what I know
I come to work, that's all there is
For some strange reason, he thinks I'm his
Think of me he does do
Watch it now, I just might sue
Obsession is his all along
What he doesn't know is
I'm so strong
Stronger than you, who are so little
Who takes after those to whom you belittle
Your face, well, now was missing teeth
Tell me, friend, what's beneath
A wicked man who quotes the Bible
Watch out, guy, you've met your rival
A righteous place I do take
All you do is play the fake

God's loving hand was with me every day
Before I went, I did pray
God, see me through this
For strength, I ask
To remove the boss
Who wears a mask
Gone from here, oh so bad
Tell ya what,
I'm not so sad.

God!

Him

A mean old man you seemed to be
You never ever looked at me
My father, you were
With me in tow
I'm this person you don't even know
A brilliant man, so they say
You saved people's lives day after day
Come and see me, I do ask
Every night you drink from the flask
First, the whiskey
and then the beer
I run to you for help, but you aren't near
How do I trust you when you refuse
You always had such a super short fuse
You look at me with those mean eyes
I'm waiting now to be chastised
Ashamed I feel for nothing I've done
Away from you I want to run
Old you are but still can't see
All along it was me
We bury you in an upstate grave
I know now of what I crave

Strength is the means in which we
Strive, to engage the courage we
Have inside

Good Night Nancy

See ya, sayonara, hit the road, Jack
So easy it is to talk this kinda smack

Please, please, please
Come back,
Will you please, Mr. Jack

I don't really mean that
But know no other than the last two
Years spent from under the cover

Away from the pain, away from the emotion
Which keeps you stuck from true forward motion

The anger which seems to consume my person
Has taken its toll, and my life has worsened

Bitterness has taken away the very person I am
Inside this shell
A true worthy gem

When will you come out,
Oh so ready to shout
This is the person,
I am really about!

Goodbye to you who held me down and
Kept my face in a perpetual frown

The world goes 'round, yes, it does
Even the lampshades turn with the sun

Goodbye to you who fooled me so
I guess I didn't really want to know
Alone I am, but my life's only steward
Oh well, for now, I must move forward

A new life I must attain
This pain, this pain, it serves me not

My new life is for me to sew
So I can learn to grow
And meet the person
I so desperately need to know!

Acceptance certainly escapes my thoughts
It seems I just prefer to live distraught
My life is not at all as imagined
When the thoughts of growing up
Were fathomed
It feels like such a betrayal
That my life should be lead this way
How is it I just can't learn
Or perhaps I just refuse to earn
The promises of our Savior
In which our lives are truly favored
I seem to be a stubborn Joe
And always wanted things just so
The willingness to let go
Has got to be the hardest thing
I want to run, and I want to sing
But I keep myself in the boxing ring
Living life just seems a fight
Maybe this time I will get it right
I want to live as you've designed
And stop myself from looking behind
Each new turn in life's events
Seem to cause me to repent
And add to the list in which I've
Created

To turn it over is a foreign
Place, over and over
I feel his grace
Finally I do see
That my God has never forsaken me

9-11-01

by Amanda Kelley

The dust and the clutter appeared miles high,
And the screams of the people
Seemed to shake even the sky.
The tears and the sobs were so dreadfully sad,
The buildings collapsed
Because people were mad.
Ignorance is fatal, and now we can see
That such blindfolded people
Can affect someone like me.
So little in this world,
I stood shocked with sorrow inside,
I mustn't stop living,
I must never hide.
The violence is over,
But the event is still lurking
Inside every heart
To try to keep us from working.
The scene continuously plays over in our heads
Because lives, dreams, and loves
Were so suddenly dead.
Don't forget what happened,
But don't be sheltered by fear.
Go out and have fun
With your friends always near.
Live your life to the fullest
Make every second count
Notice every penny
Don't focus on the doubt.
For our strengths must endure
So the success of our enemies
Shall be never more.

Our America

This flag of ours was sewn with stars
By a people who came from afar

To envision this nation
Was of God's creation
By a people who traveled to obtain
Abdication

Today it seems
We are bursting at the seams
And can't withstand
The constant demand

My rights or yours,
It makes no matter

The more they pull, the greater it's tattered

The powers that be refuse to understand
That our rights and our freedoms
From the very core
Are what keeps the America we so adore

Our nation continues in God's good grace
Because we welcome all people
of every race

But the stewards of this nation
Discovered of God's creation
Consume their time with
Taxation, inflation, and translation

The constitution stands as it was designed
Dear steward, please just keep in mind
The words which are written there
Have kept this nation from despair
This wonderful place must remain
In the race
And offer its freedoms to all who abide there

When did we the people become a
Complacent man and let every other person
Play our hand!

Let's roll!

The Light from Within

The light from within
God wants us to see
That our lives can really be free
Take from our experiences
And make them the best
God is willing to do the rest
Our light it does shine
Continue to climb
The light from within
Will never dim

About the Author

Author Nancy Kelley is an insightful, fun-loving, adventurous mother of three lovely women. She has a passion for the arts and is directed often by life events. Combining life events with poetry and art has been a gift and is created to share with the hopeful and the faithful.

This About the Author section is dedicated from my sisters, Phyllis Susan, and Mom

Nancy Jean, whose eyes are green, can meet you once,
And you've "been seen"
These poems are of what she has seen,
Mom, Dad, Sisters, Brothers, Lovers and children too,
The gifts and the lessons of life's ups and downs
Pay attention, read between the lines.
Who of us hasn't had such times?
God bless her smile,
Wit and charm,
The artistic way she uses her arm
She lights up a room, and loves to party, doesn't miss a trick and
Doesn't do tardy
Likes to laugh, likes mischief too, Nancy gullible? Well who knew?
She's famous for her Buffalo Chicken Dip,
Eat it up, it goes right quick
Nancy Jean is a generous lady, quite insightful and innovating
God gave her an adventurous spirit, one that
is certain and downright committed
She's a girly girl wearing makeup and jew-
els, but one step on her toes
And be ready to duel
Nan's work here is a gift to those who know,
Just what it takes to get on with the show

CPSIA information can be obtained
at www.ICGtesting.com
Printed in the USA
BVHW06*1101050418

512412BV00006B/6/P

9 781641 149686